The Longest Story Ever Told

Based on Daniel 8:14 and Daniel 9

Abe`-Noelle Pryce

[Handwritten: There are pictures you can color that will help you remember the story. Love Grandma Van Hise]

Note to parents:

This book features black-and-white images for your child to color.

Copyright © 2015 Abe`-Noelle Pryce
Copyright © 2015 TEACH Services, Inc.
ISBN-13: 978-1-4796-0482-1 (Paperback)
ISBN-13: 978-1-4796-0483-8 (iBooks)
ISBN-13: 978-1-4796-0484-5 (Kindle Fire)
Library of Congress Control No: 2015934578

TEACH Services, Inc.
PUBLISHING
www.TEACHServices.com • (800) 367-1844

Long ago there lived a prophet named Daniel. Daniel loved God and always prayed and studied God's Word. God loved Daniel too and talked to Him through dreams and visions.

One day God gave Daniel a vision that he could not understand. It was an important **prophecy** that spoke about events that would occur long after Daniel's time.

It was the longest **prophecy** ever told, lasting 2300 years.

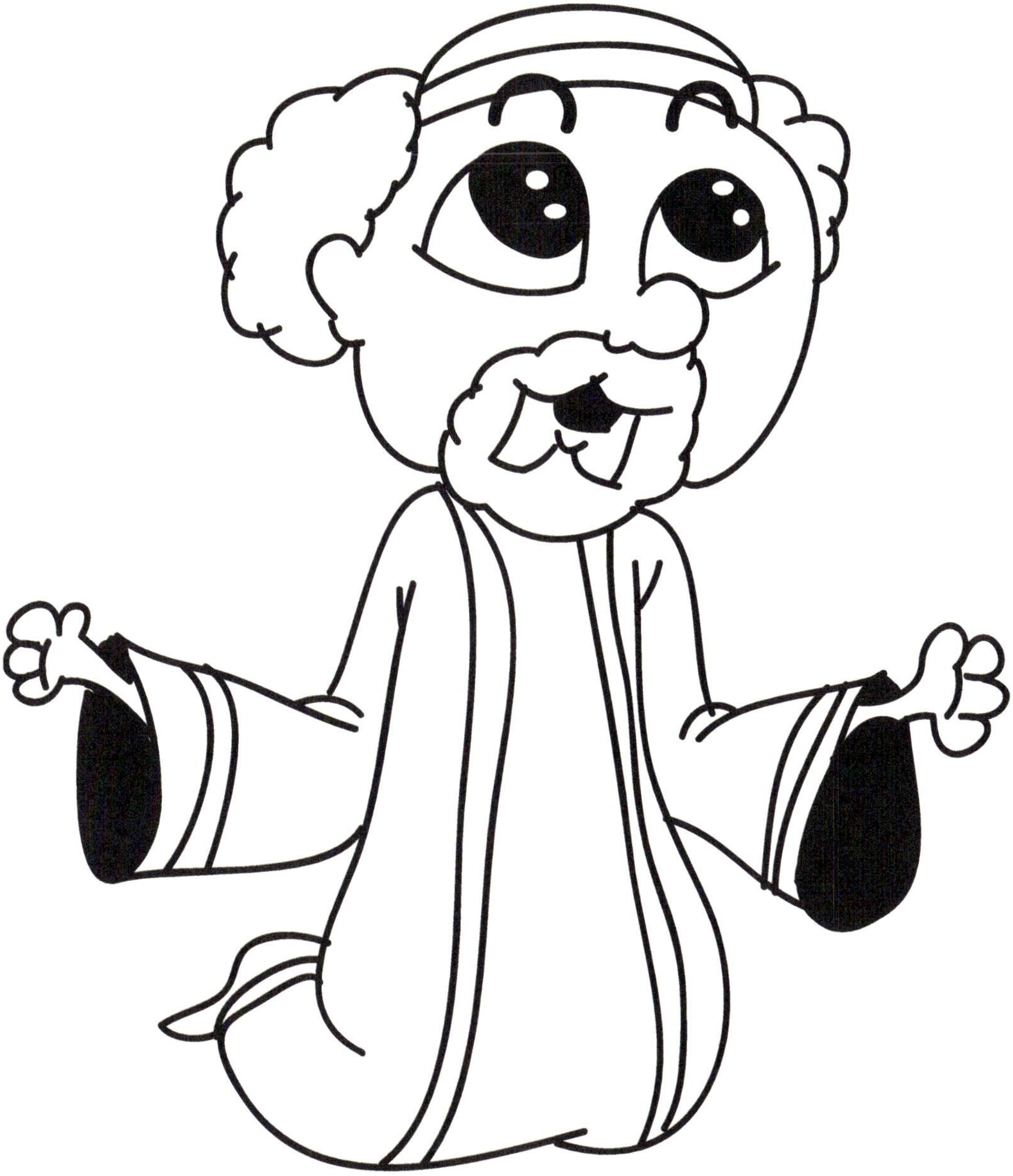

God sent an angel to explain the vision to Daniel. The angel told Daniel that 70 weeks would be cut off from the 2300 days just for the Israelites, Daniel's people.

In that time, they had to show whether they truly loved God. He wanted to know whether they would turn away from their sins and follow God. Since one day in prophecy equals one year, Israel was given 490 years out of the 2300 years to prove their loyalty to God.

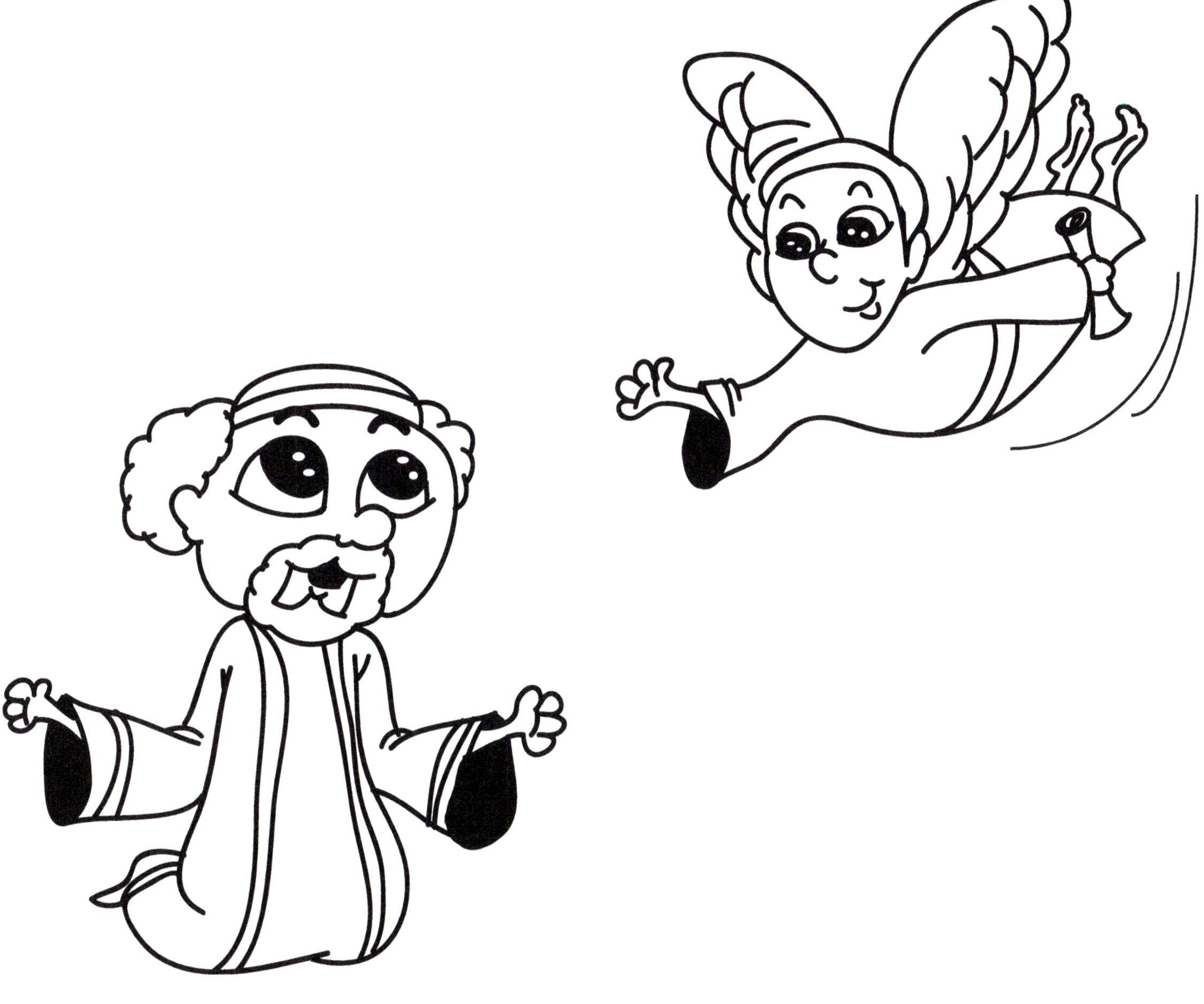

The 2300 years started when a royal command was given to restore Jerusalem. When Daniel was young, Jerusalem was destroyed, and he and his people were taken captive to Babylon. The command to restore Jerusalem was given in 457 B.C. by a Persian emperor named Artexerxes.

457 B.C.

The angel also told Daniel how long it would take for the ***restoration*** of Jerusalem to be completed—it would take 49 years. The ***restoration*** of Jerusalem was completed in 408 B.C., 49 years after the royal command of Artexerxes, just as the angel had said.

After telling Daniel about Jerusalem, the angel began to talk about Jesus. The angel told Daniel when Jesus would be baptized and when He would die, long before His parents were even born.

408 B.C.

According to the **prophecy**, Jesus would be baptized 434 years after Jerusalem had been **restored**. He would be baptized during the last "week" (which equals 7 years) of the 490 years cut off for Jerusalem

Just as the angel said, Jesus was baptised in A.D. 27, exactly 434 years after the **restoration** of Jerusalem.

A.D. 27

Right in the middle of this last "week" (which equals 7 years), the angel told Daniel that Jesus would die for us. Jesus took the punishment for our sins so we could be forgiven and live with Him forever. Just as the angel said Jesus died in the middle of the 7 years in A.D. 31.

After Jesus' death, there was one more event that would occur to end the 490 years for Israel. It happened in A.D. 34. From the royal command of Artexerxes in 457 B.C. to A.D. 34, it was exactly 490 years just as the angel had said.

A.D. 31

After Jesus died, His disciples went all around Israel teaching the people about Him. One disciple named Stephen loved to help people and preach about Jesus. But the Jewish leaders did not like hearing Stephen speak about Jesus. He was put on trial and sentenced to death. Stephen was stoned to death in A.D. 34. His stoning showed that Israel did not really love God. They had rejected Him. From this time forward, Jesus' disciples preached to the **Gentiles** all around the world.

There was only one more thing left to explain. When would the 2300 years end? In Daniel's vision, God had showed him that after the 2300 years a **sanctuary** would be cleansed. If we add 2300 years to 457 B.C. when the **prophecy** began, it brings us to the year 1844.

A.D. 34

A man named William Miller calculated all the dates you see in this book by studying the Bible. He realized that the cleansing of the **sanctuary** would fall in 1844. In that time they thought the **sanctuary** was a symbol of the earth, so William Miller thought Jesus was coming back in 1844. He told everyone about his important discovery, and lots of people waited for Jesus to come.

But Jesus did not come in 1844 like the people thought. The people were very disappointed and sad. They called this time the Great Disappointment. After the Great Disappointment, some people stopped believing in Jesus, but others continued to study the Bible. God showed them that there is a **sanctuary** in heaven. After Jesus went back to heaven, He became our **High Priest**, a job that allows Him to **intercede** on our behalf before God. In 1844 Jesus moved into the Most Holy Place in the **sanctuary** in heaven.

A.D. 1844

Since 1844 Jesus and the angels have been looking over the books in heaven. This is where all the things we have done, both good and bad, are written. When we pray to God and ask for forgiveness of our **sins**, Jesus writes forgiven beside our names and crosses out the **sin**. Jesus wants us to live with Him in heaven, but our **sins** have to be crossed out and forgiven first.

Jesus is your best friend, and you can talk to Him about anything. When you do something wrong or feel sad or when something wonderful happens to you, tell Jesus about it. No matter what, He promises to always listen to you when you pray to Him.

TODAY

CAN YOU DO THE MATH?

2300 DAYS/YEARS

A.D. 27

A.D. 34

457 B.C.

408 B.C.

A.D. 31

7 WEEKS OR _____3._____ DAYS/YEARS

3 SCORE AND 2 WEEKS (62 WEEKS) OR _____4._____ DAYS/YEARS

1 WEEK OR 7 DAYS/YEARS

70 WEEKS OR _____ DAYS/YEARS
1.

(DANIEL 9:24)

FILL IN THE BLANKS

(DANIEL 8:14)

A.D. 1844

_____ **DAYS/YEARS**
    2.

**NOTE:
1 DAY IN PROPHECY IS EQUAL TO 1 YEAR
(NUMBERS 14:34
EZEKIEL 4:6)**

"Can You Do the Math?" Answers

Remember, in prophecy 1 day = 1 year

1. Since 1 week = 7 days / 70 weeks = 7 × 70 = 490 days/years
2. Number of days/years between A.D. 1844 and A.D. 34 / 1844 − 34 = 1810 days/years
3. Since 1 week = 7 days / 7 weeks = 7 × 7 = 49 days/years
4. 1 score = 20 / 3 score = 60 / 3 score + 2 = 62 / 62 weeks = 7 × 62 = 434 days/years

How To Calculate Dates From Timeline

Here are two things to note when calculating dates from the timeline:
- In B.C. we count down, so we subtract. In A.D. we count up, so we add.
- There is no 0 year (0 B.C. or A.D. 0), 1 B.C. is followed by A.D. 1.

457 B.C.

Counting down from 457 B.C. by 49 days/years = 457 − 49 = 408 B.C
From 408 B.C. to 1 B.C. = 408 years
Years left to count up after B.C. 1 = 434 − 408 = 26

⬇

Adding extra year (A.D. 1) = A.D. 27

⬇

Middle/half of 1 week = 3 ½ years
A.D. 27 + 3 ½ = A.D. 30 ½ or A.D. 31

⬇

A.D. 27 + 7 years (1 week) = A.D. 34

⬇

A.D. 34 + 1810 years = A.D. 1844

Definition of Key Terms (in bold)

Prophecy: Messages that tell us about the future. God gave these messages to people called prophets so they could warn His people.

Sin: The bad things we do or think about that are against God's commandments.

Restoration: Repairing something that has been damaged so it can be like it was before being damaged.

Gentiles: In Bible times this term referred to anyone who was not from Israel/people who were not Jewish

Sanctuary: In Israel the sanctuary was where all the people went to bring gifts to God and ask for forgiveness of their sins. Once a year the high priest would go into a part of the sanctuary called the Most Holy Place. In this place all the sins that the people had asked for forgiveness of throughout the year were symbolically cleaned and removed from the sanctuary, signifying that all the people were truly forgiven. There is a sanctuary in heaven that Jesus is serving in right now, cleansing us of our sins.

High Priest: This was the main religious leader of Israel. The high priest worked in the sanctuary/temple. He offered the gifts of the people to God so they could be forgiven, and he talked to God on their behalf. Jesus is working right now as High Priest in the sanctuary in heaven.

Intercede/Intercession: Whenever we do something wrong and ask for forgiveness, Jesus speaks to God for us so we can be forgiven. He talks about His death and how He took the punishment for sin so we don't need to.

We invite you to view the complete
selection of titles we publish at:

www.TEACHServices.com

Scan with your mobile
device to go directly
to our website.

Please write or e-mail us your praises, reactions, or thoughts about this or any other book we publish at:

TEACH Services, Inc.
P U B L I S H I N G
www.TEACHServices.com • (800) 367-1844

P.O. Box 954
Ringgold, GA 30736

info@TEACHServices.com

TEACH Services, Inc., titles may be purchased in bulk for educational, business, fund-raising, or sales promotional use. For information, please e-mail:

BulkSales@TEACHServices.com

Finally, if you are interested in seeing your own book in print, please contact us at

publishing@TEACHServices.com

We would be happy to review your manuscript for free.

CPSIA information can be obtained at www.ICGtesting.com
Printed in the USA
LVOW05s1209180915

454739LV00011B/20/P